Drops of Rain

/

Drops of Wine

Patrick James Dunagan

SPUYTEN DUYVIL
New York City

Acknowledgements

Portions of this poem appeared earlier with *Dusie* and *Forklift*, many thanks to editors Carrie Hunter and Matt Hart, respectfully.

©2016 Patrick James Dunagan
ISBN 978-1-941550-99-1
Cover image: Gary Lee Dunagan, Vietnam
[Date unknown, photographer unknown]

Library of Congress Cataloging-in-Publication Data

Names: Dunagan, Patrick James, author.
Title: Drops of rain/drops of wine / Patrick James Dunagan.
Description: New York City : Spuyten Duyvil, [2016]
Identifiers: LCCN 2015044645 | ISBN 9781941550991
Classification: LCC PS3604.U497 A6 2016 | DDC 811/.6--dc23
LC record available at http://lccn.loc.gov/2015044645

for Gary Dunagan

I don't write songs ... that's a whole other concept ... I just make them up.
                    Janis Joplin

    What'll
          we say

your old man's
        gonna go

  knock the
       sky

/

breaks
      in myth

  who & what

 won

    nothing sacred

      you see
     the spirit
    spilling out like
horses   in waves   cross
               the plains

/

Great Expenditures
by M. Price

$12 to "Susie"
@ Great Clips in
       Boulder
          (no tip

/

too much death

        what

    is this?

      Old

      mystical now

          this is November
                in which
            we walk

   watch

/

"ego like a lantern"

no beauty in that

or <u>story</u>

/

      talking shit
           hoped would
  walk

/

John Clare hiding out in tree trunks
                that he might write
                              un-judged

/

get centered

/

        what is this?

this is what's there

/

too many clichés

        pain of

white eyes

        the enduring love

affair

/

    writing fades

            only the reading
         continues

               before
                    the page

        as so
               past
           the page

               breathing life

    into
          pressed ink

/

THE GREAT WESTERN

                                           open form

                       living out the art

                              pays in alcohol &
                                      tobacco

/

"keep your sould

        let me find a chicken"

/

    this history

        "most can't even
                ride
            forget about
        knowing something *not*
            yourself"

/

maps of peoples
   scattered
across his face

/

two things
        happening at once
                what's seen
                      is done

/

to live
in a thousand
worlds
not one
a home

/

DOLPHY TIME

    lovely twitter
    down Masonic

    each line
    comes in
    about right

    this time
    of year

    the birds
    jez doin'
    their thing

    in San Francisco

    it's lovely
    listening
          in

                    for Jeffrey Butler

/

Love, he said,
   will eat away the empire
   until chaos remains.
          Robert Duncan

    lovely twitter
      the birds   the
        birds
                down Masonic
       twitter

lovely
   how
  the
 birds
    go

   each line
   about right

the birds
  this year   the

   birds
  just
        doing

                    their
                              thing
           down Masonic
                    the birds

                 each line
                 drops
                    coming
                 in
                          just
                       right

           lovely twitter
                    of the birds
      the
          measured song
             they sing

  skips
    as
 they
   do
   branch
        to
      branch

                    the birds   the
               twitter
                  coming
           down

      along
      Masonic
      this year

it's lovely
      hearing
    that
           Other City
      come alive
           so

    listening
          in

                "the birds are junk"

for Jeffrey, again

/

it's like

you can't explain

a joke

you can't explain

jazz

you do it

cuz it's FUN

the excitement

of doing IT

      Philip Whalen

/

a welcomed violence

/

knowing who you are

        what it is

your writing
    goes
  where intended

           or not

thought anyway
      finds way

/

        beside the pool
                naked
            drink in hand
urging others on
              how live with
                    that
        iconic cinema boner

              !?!

        THE BIG STARS

    chewing
              on words
        white on red
                jagged font

/

to hold
possibility

nailing it
down

fer a sec

/

who walks
        between
                the winds
            nobody
                bothers
                      translate

/

it doesn't come easy

it just comes

/

      anybody
    can be a cowboy
              some Indian
         a Bugs Bunny
                  Show

            w/ swaggering step
  belt
        low slung
                  off hip

/

just something

that's FUN to do

it or not

And makes me

very nervous

not to be doing it

        Philip Whalen

/

glyph

cypher

mark

/

erasure

    identity
of being
  a human
  thing
    older
      than
  rock

        stone & stream
                memory walks

/

    possible
      'what is'
  state of
        becoming
   as much
         as
    as not

/

    one's haunt   not haunted
        make the time yr own

                never easy to arrive
        self never   fully   recognized

doing anything well requires   presence
    a gift   numerous thing   to know

                for Neeli Cherkovski

/

we're having

a linguistic relationship

right now

& it's obviously

ambiguous

    Philip Lamantia

/

Reading Skull Face
        on the Big Vegetable

"I just want to wreck your mind"

    how do that / instruction
                manual
              for the sane literate

    zonked out
      on reality

    grasping the opportunity

…his seemingly
      Just Writing
    absorbs
      the activity—

          gone in a minute—

/

'nothing'

/

    inherent romanticism
        of poetry
   inescapable
       fact of

              ours

/

    that
'social syntax'
    is what song
                's all
      bout

      communal
      sure
        at core
      what else
        are bodies
          for?
              being

    after all
      exactly
    what is

/

    a deck of Tarot

    tossed to the
             air

fallen
        where it may
            lies

        leaving

    nothing but
        lifts
            of wind

            departs as day
                approaches

/

Aether

   "the ultimate ground

      on which anything moves"

/

slips in
    sequence

      light
  airy
        nooks

/

speaking against
skull-racket
mirrored verse
echo of others
moving away from
assembling knowledge
no goal
other than
hearing
what outside's
far from perfection

/

> *you could turn*
> *the soul*
> *into a page*
>   David Meltzer

to be moving)
　　a necessary advantage—

...a discipline he had not
　　created, a mere
　　obedience...

　　W.B. Yeats

crooks & hustlers
　hustlers &
　　crooks
　Dickens Universe

　　　so much less
　than what's
　　　worth

guides the hand
　every fate
knows
　　what awaits

/

    to give a shit about anything
           these questions (are they
        questions worth thinking about

the investigation of personality
                        chore of refusal
        a lifetime learning
                       experiences

/

*after a poetry reading by
Nick Whittington & Jack Hirschman*

there is but one Song

that is joy

comes as it does

anonymously

or not at all

you share it

right away

else risk

perish eternal

      no joke

/

    unreal becoming
             necessity
       to pass on
                forms
             which honor
         repeat appearance
                  everybody
            in chaos

/

there's no accounting

>   bad blue news
>   what to do—
>   nothing's changing

 a distant hurt
  immediate
            unannounced arrives
         unwelcomed

 the way it is
 no changing
 caught up
 within past
 doing

 days behind
 years

 suffered thru
 forced ahead
 to get here

            with everything

                        in tow

        how
  less than by doing
    transform

              yourself into
              another
              you'd recognize
              by friendly wager

  to tempt
  a few more years
  worth living
  out of

(here wanting
    casual weight

      such results
    no refusal assures
          services
      another'd not

likewise fail

    what's what

  remains

      no changing

[Oct-Jan, 2011-12]

II. [Jan. 28-Feb. 5, 2012]

Still at it
imperious

/

and we with profligates' complete sashay
set brandy on the table and slapped down the grass
                    Kenneth Irby

        resting my bourbon
        gentle as a doll—
        like the lady called
        Av when shopping
        @ Christina's work—
        the other hand's
        easy slap
        comes off the page
        as I read

        going back over
        after voices
        left
        missed through the years
        not searching
        anything specific

                just letting the feel
                        wash in
                    for all its worth

jumbled
but felt
through and through

don't go breakin' it
forgettin' it or
later regrettin' it

Bar Rules for your Too Late
                        Millennial Blues

/

    O   dreamer of
                  Song
        tell

            where
                  is it
        headed

    the living
force
        compels
    all of this

          even beaten

                  in essence
    doing
    nothing

            live with it
                awhile
        you'll see
          how it is

   merely being
        your vision
                continues

/

        the page
holds its own charms
                these things
    drift
            all round us

      what are you
   doing
         why don't
      you locate
           yourself

/

        hint
fabricate
    mystify

            (yourself most of all

/

don't understand
or know
this won't
hold true
unless you
remain most
dedicated as
un original
you're able

/

tell the story
    not myth
        of who
    and what
        where
    and when
      so done

  even if
   simply
   adding
       to the jumble

/

looking to locate
the situation
we're in

    to have legends
to look out of

    not rise
up any hordes
    in pride
swell no
    desirous core

fuck that

. . .

/

    eyes
  a world
      yet beyond
  awaits hearing

knocks the page
          brings
      sky
      to hand

            an answer

there is no
answer

nothing's forgotten
    . . .   forgiven
    . . .   left

only movement lasts

/

    left with a bunch
           of worthless
         shit

      somebody else
      in a state of
      loss

        claims
        ideas
        un-thought

     passed down
     by example

set us
apart

    to-
   gether
   on our
      way

paths which unite us
that words break   paths
through burnt out territory
which outlast us   betrayal our only
              constant worry

/

sometimes writing

is simply (or not

just that thing

all its own

/

    going along
just discovering
        what might be next

/

   poets

       dig

write

shit

down

     now

   & then

/

the whole world is Father
                Ana Božičević

>   never to have
>   enough of
>   him   this mother
>   of a job
>   life's doing
>
>   forget about
>   <u>any</u> solution
>   there's plenty
>   heartless care
>   worth listening
>
>   demands you know
>   nothing

/

    busy   constructing
        vast distraction

these night raids
        of turmoil
    in the heart

        deep rooted

these   the hours
        no profit
    rises out of

        absence
          (a declaration
        vacates the premises
            itself

    states
        no-
    body
  minds

        one
          long
    peel
        from here to

  getting somewhere
you say you was "one time when…"

/

    your person is
that other you   burned
       out on being
          held to

/

there's a story

    o   there's

always

        a story

      told to no avail

/

pulling
at ends while
in the middle of avoiding
just being
where you're at

never to pick an economy

not an exercise

frivolous living

<u>costs</u>

/

too few memories

        to mask

any regrets

      heavy blanket
of smoke
           over eggs &
      potatoes

      pancakes
          w/ coffee
   cocoa beside
         vast array of syrup

international haunt
where we hang out

/

we've walked
as talk ebbed

/

faces peeled back
no paints replace

/

    a lover's distance
        this isn't

easy familiarity
   of a tug
eases you back

recognizing myself
      here

/

    many people spend much of their rime
      being certain they're misremembering
everything and everybody as much as possible

                it's a form of protection
                perhaps
                        of valuing
                relationships
                        over accuracy

/

skipping rocks
hilt to hilt
Pacific moon-backed
clear mid nite middle of
day
alphabetized and color-coded
reading the rules
chalked up in laughter
marks water don't hold
highway 1 never misses
we float over all

beach days spent w/
Micah Ballard and Christina Fisher

/

borrow a little
rethink a lot

/

any hope of balance
proves rot
trust fails love
there's never room
or air enough
song abandons the stories
a silence I refuse learn
taught over and over
all I'll ever know
confused hurt I just
walk away from

/

everything comes down to who you are
             where you from what
          your folks learned you
                       or didn't
                whether you know enough
                   to be silly
           with a lover or not
                    you know you can't ever
              knock it off
                     this mask borne
                 is all the you you'll know
                 ain't no fate
                          way it is is the way
                                             it is

/

        any challenges

     not weathered through

            beat the living shit

out of you

/

survival
      or rather
   self-
      ish   interests
get in way of
        care

    forget everything
    else

    you have yourself

/

there is no conversation

silence bores through all

/

      pettiness   so drab

           honestly

      how self-centered

                to get away

with yourself unawares

not the right word

          off on your own

      so many years

          never mind

   feeling

      responsible

*

        enough

    to knock

           the head

     clear off!

/

<u>holidays</u>

forget 'bout
knowing

who isn't
steppin'

thru the
door

during those
culture

wars our
kind

drinks thru

/

foolish most to any want to give love
Kennth Irby

    how benefit
       from
    spell it out

        another

whose only
      act

  is one
      of

      absence

what's significant
  why
      take the
  bother

```
        you
  refuse what
    for better
                or otherwise
        any other than
            you
                too well
                    knows
```

/

      memory is descriptive

          the unsaid

hollow

     sounds of

being wherever

       whenever

/

      you live

   you who would

          hear

       in absence

           dry sorrow

/

go on

go

make your mark

/

        have your fill
pleasure
        all you're able
   for tomorrow
          surely
            arrives with
                more of
       the same

  a constant rush
      this river
    picks you
      carves its own path
   guide
       more deliberate than
    you'll ever
           understand

CODA:

I don't got
nothin' to say

jez go away

\\

serious-
    ly
  nothin'
     to say

heartsick
words don't
do no trick

\\

hangin' round
jez danglin'

round afta
round

itsa real
az itsa
happenin'
rite now

\\

now go get
ta figurin'
er, rather, don't
none of yr bizness
ya know how I mean
itsa none
of yr bizness
pal

this ain't thru

ah, yes it is

is it thru

oh, yes it is

\\

is ain't is

'cept so

II.

Inner smile
Ring phone
Droopies
             Ted Greenwald

No
"ring phone/Droopies"
nothing like that
yr hangin' round
ten more years
comes as no
more a surprise
than ten less

\\

No Foolin' Jez Bullshittin'

anything'll show
itself
come tomorrow
or today

only writing it down
threatens stall
any event
from happening

all depends on
things being
just so
doin' what they do

that damn sun
just *has* to
for fuck's sake
so do that moon

\\\\

So Long

>Only

>Goodbye

>Cell

>Throbbing

>All

>Night

\\

Gregory Corso's
poems/are egg
   beaters
     for shit
              Joanne Kyger

   fathers come in
   whatever form
   fathers come

\\

only an asshole

    writes just 3 poems

a year

    but you

    you don't write

but one letter

    a lifetime

\\

So Cal Blues

        mom's
           a valley girl

      dad's
          Venice-Santa Monica
          spoiled
         by way of
              Nebraska

his mother's early death / his father's love debt

\\

   I'll scatter your ashes
  next to both
    in Albion

\\

there's only
unanswered
song

[Feb. 29, 2012]

PATRICK JAMES DUNAGAN lives in San Francisco and works at Gleeson Library for the University of San Francisco. A graduate of the Poetics program from the now-defunct New College of California he's currently helping to edit an anthology of critical writings by Poetics program alumni and faculty. He also edited and wrote the introduction for poet Owen Hill's *A Walk Among the Bogus* (Lavender Ink). His essays and book reviews appear frequently with a wide number of both online and print publications. His most recent books include: *"There are people who think that painters shouldn't talk": A Gustonbook* (Post Apollo), *Das Gedichtete* (Ugly Duckling), and *from Book of Kings* (Bird and Beckett Books).

www.ingramcontent.com/pod-product-compliance
Lightning Source LLC
Chambersburg PA
CBHW020944090426
42736CB00010B/1253